**Habitat Explorer**

# Rivers, Ponds and Lakes

## Nick Baker

Collins

I dedicate this book to my friend Sue Daniells, an adult who should know better!
For many fascinating hours pouring through the sludge in the bottom of
countless pond nets.

First published in 2006 by
Collins, an imprint of
HarperCollinsPublishers
77-85 Fulham Palace Road
Hammersmith
London W6 8JB

www.collins.co.uk

Collins is a registered trademark of HarperCollins Publishers Ltd

12 11 10 09 08 07 06
7 6 5 4 3 2 1

Editorial director: Helen Brocklehurst
Editor: Emma Callery
Designer: Sue Miller
Photographer: Nikki English, except for those pictures credited below
Flick book illustrations: Lizzie Harper
Editorial assistant: Julia Koppitz
Production: Graham Cook

ISBN 0-00-720764-6
ISBN -13 978-0-00-720764-0

Colour Reproductions by Dot Gradations Ltd, UK
Printed and bound in Hong Kong by Printing Express

Photograph credits (b = bottom, l = left, m = middle, r = right, t = top)
Page 5: © Wil Meinderts/Foto Natura/FLPA; 13 (t, bl), 20: © Nicholas Phelps Brown/Nature Photographers Ltd;
13 (br), 18, 23 (bl, r), 27 (t), 34, 38, 42, 47 (tr, bl), 57 (b), 63 (ml), 65 (t), 67: © Paul Sterry/Nature Photographers Ltd;
16, 29 (b), 35 (r): © S C Bisserot/Nature Photographers Ltd; 23 (t): © Alan Williams/NHPA; 23 (m): © Norbert
Wu/FLPA; 26 (l): © A E Bonsall/Nature Photographers Ltd; 26 (r), 47 (br), 59 (tr): © Geoff du Feu/Nature
Photographers Ltd; 27 (l): © John Shaw/NHPA; 27 (r): © R Sorensen & J Olsen/NHPA; 28, 29 (t): © Duncan
Usher/Foto Natura/FLPA; 37: © Acres Wild/Ian Smith; 39 (tl, br), 41 (br): © Stephen Dalton/NHPA; 39 (tr): © Foto
Natura Stock/FLPA; 39 (bl): © George Bernard/NHPA; 40: © Heather Angel/Natural Visions; 41 (bl): © George
Bernard/NHPA; 48: © Martin B Withers/FLPA; 52: © Hugh Miles/Nature Photographers Ltd; 56: © Philip
Newman/Nature Photographers Ltd; 57 (tl): © Mike Lane/NHPA; 65 (b): © Cisca Castelijns/Foto Natura/FLPA.

# Contents

## Freshwater habitats 4

Flick the pages to see the tadpole grow!

# Freshwater habitats

Life needs water and so wherever water accumulates on the planet's surface, life tends to concentrate; whether it's something as temporary as a puddle or as vast as the ocean. In this book I concentrate the naturalists' explorations on those readily available pools of freshwater – puddles, ponds, rivers and bogs – focusing on ways to explore the moist worlds and the creatures they contain.

**There is no supply of new water on our planet:** the water we use has been used and re-used for millions of years. When water is heated it evaporates (like steam from a boiling kettle) and rises until it cools and turns into clouds. These clouds burst when they get too heavy, releasing their vapour as rain falling to the ground. This flows into rivers, lakes and seas, from where the whole cycle starts again.

**From puddles to lakes, ditches to rivers,** bogs to mires and water butt to fish tank, each contains a whole world of the weird and wonderful, unusual and fascinating. Whether you choose to dive into all the activities I have pulled together from years of being an avid pond dipper or whether you are just looking for a cool way to spend an afternoon, hopefully a page or two will catch your imagination and you will never look at a frog or a water beetle in the same way again!

**Different kinds of freshwater attract different kinds of life,** which have tuned their lifestyles and body shapes to the challenges that each habitat contains. Life in a pond may look similar to life in a stream – and there may well be overlap for some animals and plants – but look closer and more often than not, the animals and plants differ quite a lot from one another.

**The differences are reflected within the pages of this book** and broken down into corresponding chapters that deal with each. Many of the activities, however, are not necessarily exclusive to each habitat, so go out with this thought in your mind: 'Eyes peeled, mind open and net and jam jar ready' – and enjoy getting wet and muddy.

It doesn't have to be a natural water body to be of interest to wildlife; a simple water butt or a cattle trough will appeal just as much.

A boggy bit of land, swamp and marsh may not have much water that is obvious, but the puddles that do exist are often home to some very rare and specialized creatures that can handle the slightly more acidic conditions.

This slow-moving mill pond has a rich growth of water weeds and is home to a mixed bunch of animals, some of which are found in both flowing and still water.

# A bag of holes!

**Naturalists and nets go together like sharks and teeth!** They are simply very useful extensions to the human body and allow us to touch places that would otherwise be hard to reach. Nets become the means by which we enter another world. Because of this, there is a responsibility and a code of conduct that should be followed to avoid unnecessary suffering and discomfort to your subjects.

**Whatever net you are using,** at some point you will have to lift it clear of the water. As soon as the water has drained through the holes, any living things in the net are going to start feeling uncomfortable. So handle and sort the contents as soon as possible. Some creatures, such as adult water insects, are OK for quite some time but other creatures, such as fish and tadpoles, need water to breathe and will also dry out and dehydrate very quickly.

**You must make sure EVERY living creature** is happy and reasonably content submerged in water – in tubs, buckets, pots and trays – before you start observing any of them.

**Nets are invaluable to the water naturalist, but you need to use them in conjunction with a tray or tub. This is so you can sort through what, at first hand, often appears to be nothing but a mass of sludge.**

**Once you have got a net full of good stuff**, it can seem a little daunting peering into the mud, muck and weed and this is where a white tray comes in handy. As soon as you have removed your net from the water, support the bag with one hand and carefully turn it inside out into your white tray already filled with water.

**It may still look like a bit of a mess**, but spread everything out and let it settle down and from the murk you will start noticing movements as a dragonfly larva stumbles out of the silt or a worm starts wiggling! Now you can start redistributing various creatures into other pots for observation.

**Remember to separate predators from prey** as in close confines creatures cannot necessarily escape and you end up with a gladiator-style showdown. Not pleasant.

**Do not leave specimens in the sun** as water temperatures will rise very quickly. As this happens, not only will your creatures – which are totally your responsibility – start to cook, but long before that the water will lose its oxygen and creatures that use gills to breathe will start to suffocate.

## Take my advice

* Pond dipping is more than sticking your net in the water and stirring everything up! In fact, doing this is one of the most common mistakes you can make. When approaching any water, keep quiet and move slowly and you can be rewarded with a shy fish basking in the shallows, a frog resting at the surface, a heron fishing or even a nervous water vole.

* Once at the water's edge, stop and peer into the water to get an idea of what sort of animals you might catch. You may even be able to gently catch an individual there and then without causing too much disturbance.

* Only once you have assessed the habitat is it time to dip your net – gently and carefully. Keep water flowing through the net's mesh. Move it slowly through the water, but not so slowly that even the slowest beetle can swim out the way it came in! A figure-of-eight pattern is perfect.

# Handy stuff: making a net

**You can buy a purpose-made net** and there are many different kinds to choose from, but it is fairly easy to make your own basic one, which will then be useful in most situations.

**The two most important ingredients of a net** are the netting itself and the wire surround. For the netting, you want something that is white and of a reasonably fine mesh. White is best because with a dark mesh, too many creatures, even the ones with bad eyesight, stand a chance of seeing you coming!

**The holes in your net** must be big enough to let the water pass through and drain out easily, but at the same time not so big that all the little creatures get through. It also needs to be robust, otherwise you will forever be replacing the torn bag. I find a tough, coarse cotton fabric is one of the easiest and most practical types of fabric to work with.

**Because the wire needs to survive a bit of a bashing,** it is best to use a heavy-duty wire that takes a bit of effort to shape. The shape of the net mouth is entirely up to you  some people like to have a flat edge, which makes working along the bottom of a pond or river easier. You could otherwise choose to make a circular one.

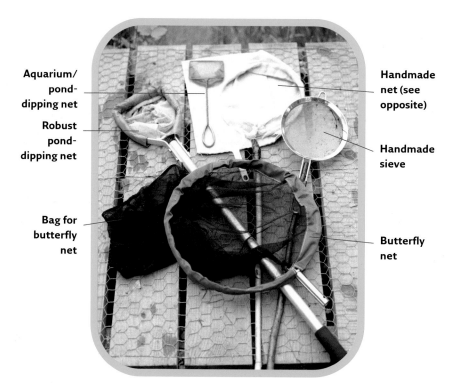

Aquarium/pond-dipping net

Robust pond-dipping net

Bag for butterfly net

Handmade net (see opposite)

Handmade sieve

Butterfly net

**1** Decide on the depth of your net. Aim for it being about as deep as it is wide and allow extra fabric to fold over at the top a couple of times. Stitch the turned-down fabric to make a channel. Fold the fabric in half. Stitch along the bottom and up the open side as far as the channel and turn the inside out.

**2** Thread the wire through the channel at the top of the bag. For size, you should aim for 20–30cm across. Anything bigger may seem like a better way of catching more, but get a big net full of weed and mud and nobody but Mr Universe would be able to haul the thing in!

**3** Cut off the excess wire so that you are left with 7.5cm sticking out at each end. You might want to ask an adult to help you with this next bit – twist together the ends of wire. Pliers can be helpful.

**4** Push them into the end of the bamboo cane and ...

**5** ... use a good length of gaffer tape to keep the cane in place. Now you're ready to dip!

# Handy stuff for exploring with

**A naturalist needs nets** and they come in different sizes and styles for different jobs. A stout-framed one with coarse netting is perfect as a pond-dipping net; a lighter one with a delicate mesh is handy for catching winged creatures. A butterfly net is useful for catching ... well, butterflies!

**Binoculars** These are expensive and one of the few things that you cannot make yourself. But they are well worth the investment and there are many prices to meet different purses. They are especially useful for bird watching, but a close focusing pair are brilliant for watching dragonflies.

**Bucket** Great for the bigger stuff.

**Magnifying lens** Another bit of kit that is worth buying. It will turn a mite into a monster.

**Plastic pots, trays and plastic aquariums** Brilliant for sorting, separating and observing your catches or collecting your specimens in. The clear ones are even more useful in a watery environment as they let you look at the animals from under the surface. Bags are handy lightweight alternatives to pots; they are also useful for keeping plant specimens fresh.

**Sieves and tea strainers** These are very handy for smaller, close-up work and sorting out creatures once you have caught them. Make them even more useful by strapping the handle to a bamboo cane with gaffer tape (see page 8), rather like the yogurt pot on a stick on page 31.

**Stout stick** I find this useful as an extra leg, especially when wading. You can use it to test the water's depth or if you are leaning out with your net, a stick is something that you can lean on for support. With a little tape or string, you can construct a makeshift net handle, too.

**Wellie boots** Okay, so they aren't fashionable, but they are a lot cooler than a shoe full of squelchy water or mud.

Pond net

Sieves

Magnifying lenses

Binoculars

Butterfly net

Back pack

Plastic aquarium

Pots/jars

Wellie boots

Stout stick

Bucket

# Puddles

Have you ever left a bucket of water out in the garden or peered into a water butt and noticed it full of wiggly things? Life has appeared as if by magic where before there was none. But this is far from a spontaneous happening. What you have just seen is the wonderfully efficient way that nature has of seeking out and colonizing a new habitat. Even a puddle, assuming it doesn't just evaporate before things get going, can be home to all manner of weird and exciting life forms.

**Try this experiment.** It is called Thienemann's tank and is named after a German scientist who first noticed this phenomena in his garden. Mr Thienemann set out to look at how aquatic invertebrates (that's to say, those animals without a backbone that live in water) colonize watery habitats. He left a tank of water in his garden and then every now and again checked it for life. Over eight years he recorded 103 species, which turned up without any aid.

**Many species, such as mites and snails,** can hitch a lift on others, and some, such as beetles, bugs and dragonflies, all at some stage in their lifetime have wings that enable them to disperse and colonize fresh habitat. But some of Mr Thienemann's finds were totally aquatic – they could only survive in water. So how did they get there?

**If you try Thienemann's experiment,** you will be creating a new habitat. The method is simple – take as big a tank or tub as possible and fill it with water. Then check it every week and record everything you see living in the water. You will almost certainly need the help of a good field guide or even your local museum to help you identify everything.

**You must also look very carefully** as some of the creatures will be very small and not at all obvious at first glance. If you have a hand lens or a microscope, this may come in very useful. Try to keep a diary. Draw pictures of anything that arrives and add the date when you noticed it.

Some amphibians, particularly toads, can breed in surprisingly small puddles of water.

Water fleas, or daphnia, are not fleas at all; they just twitch and jump about like them. They are one of the most common of the freshwater crustaceans.

Mosquito larvae are very quick to colonize tiny little puddles and pools of trapped water. The contents of water butts, old car tyres, even jam jars, soon start to twitch with the eggs, larvae and pupae of this infamous insect.

Water boatmen, like many adult water insects, actually have wings folded away and are excellent aeronauts. This means they are some of the first colonizers of a new pond, magically appearing, seemingly out of nowhere.

# Aeronauts and aquanauts

**Now you can understand how tiny little things** like water fleas can turn up in a puddle, but what about larger pond life, such as beetles, water boatmen and pond skaters? If you look in a newly dug pond or a cattle trough, you are more than likely to see a multi-eyed, six-legged water bug go rowing past. How did it get there? Well, wonder no more; the answer is that it arrived by air. To prove this, follow the steps opposite.

**Some aptly named water boatmen - their back legs look like oars and bodies like hulls.**

## Fab facts

* These insects are thought to be very sensitive to the kind of light that is reflected off the surface of water, such as ponds, lakes and streams. So when they go buzzing about above us in the air, how do they find their new home? It turns out they are able to see the light as it is reflected from the water's surface.

* The sad thing is that this worked perfectly well before mankind came along and confused things! Car bonnets and roofs look similar to water as they reflect the same kind of light and many pond insects, including water boatmen and water beetles, try to touch down in our car parks and on our roads – both fairly unfriendly places to end up dazed and spinning on your back!

**1** A big water boatman is an ideal insect to catch. It is big, so you can observe it a lot easier, and it is also easy to identify as an adult. Water boatmen are the ones with the silvery white backs, which is easy to see when they are flipping around in your net.

**2** Gently remove the insect from the net. Try to lift it without squeezing, as it can deliver a painful bite with its stabbing mouth parts. Hold it in the flat palm of your hand. It may leap about a bit at first, but it isn't in pain, or suffocating – trust me!

**3** It will soon settle down with it's back facing up, so watch it carefully. The next bit usually happens in a couple of minutes, depending on how sunny or hot it is. Watch for it to open the top of its back and start pumping its abdomen back and forth. Any second now, the boatman will unfold its wings and buzz off to find a new pond. The mystery is solved – most adult bugs have leathery wings and are good fliers. This is handy as they can check out new homes, or simply make the most of temporary ones!

## *Take it further*

* This is just a fun little experiment that helps us know how water boatmen, also known as backswimmers, orientate themselves in their underwater world.

* Take a small jar of water with your boatman in it to a dark room. Turn out the lights and shine a torch in the jar from underneath. What happens? Your water boatman – and here you must remember its other common name – has become a front swimmer. This proves they use light direction to orientate themselves in the water and not gravity.

# Handy stuff: an aquarium

**Scooping some strange and alien life forms** out of the water, looking at them for a few minutes in a tray and then putting them back can be just a little dissatisfying. Yes, if you are lucky, you may see gills twitch, a bit of scrabbling around and, if you are a good naturalist, you may be able to put a name to the creature. But surely there is more to their lives than just that? How fast do they grow? How do they eat? Do they change colour? What do they turn into?

**With just a bit of knowledge** about how to set up an aquarium properly you can take a little piece of the pond or stream and some chosen subjects back home with you. It is only by gazing into their wondrous little lives day in, day out that you really get to know them and study them properly.

**Remember, however, that once any living creature** has been lifted out of its home in your net, it is your responsibility. Be sure not to over-stock your tank and not to mix predators with prey as almost certain carnage will result. It's all about balance. Try to resist having too many individuals of any one species. One or two snails are good, but if they get happy, they will breed and eat all your plants. Lots of predatory fish or beetles look good, but may kill other, more delicate, creatures.

**Do your research about the food requirement** of your captives and look after them. If they are not looking happy, then you are probably doing something wrong. If this is the case, release your inmates back where they came from and think about your set-up. Adjust the tank accordingly and try again with fresh specimens.

Here is the great pond snail - it's looking great indeed.

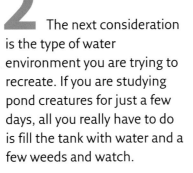

**1** A water-tight tank with clear sides is the minimum requirement. I prefer glass ones as they do not scratch or discolour, but they can chip, crack or smash if you are not gentle, and plastic ones are so much cheaper, lighter and readily available.

**2** The next consideration is the type of water environment you are trying to recreate. If you are studying pond creatures for just a few days, all you really have to do is fill the tank with water and a few weeds and watch.

**3** But if you are keeping your creatures for any longer, some gentle filtration and water circulation is a good idea. This keeps the water from becoming stagnant, ups the oxygen levels and removes and prevents a build-up of harmful substances. All this can be provided by an in-tank filter pump, again relatively cheap and available in many sizes, depending on the size of the tank it needs to filter. For species that live in running water, you may need to have quite an aggressive water flow, but the principles are the same.

**4** Use rain water or water from where you got your creatures. Tap water can be used, but as there is added chlorine, it needs to stand for a few days before putting in your catch. Ideally, set up your aquarium a week in advance of adding them.

# Make a micro zoo

**The thing about ponds and lakes** is that they are busy with life. Because they are so chock-a-block, competition for resources, like space and food, is intense. Puddles, on the other hand, tend to dry up from time to time and so are relatively empty. Now, to any creature this represents a challenge: to get life in a puddle licked you must have a speedy life cycle. You must be able to adapt so you can handle the extreme and often rapid changes in temperatures as well as sometimes very salty conditions. Do this, and you have the place pretty much to yourself.

**Yes, puddle life is tough.** But there are some creatures that have become puddle specialists. A couple of groups, such as the tadpole shrimps (or triops) and the brine shrimps, are rare in the wild in Europe, but they can be bred in captivity relatively easily. This means that you do not have to go out looking for them, but can actually buy them as eggs (see page 71) and rear them as a micro zoo or go pond dipping and see what you can catch (see opposite).

**In the wild, these animals whizz through their life** as soon as rain water fills the dents and the depressions that become puddles. They grow and filter out any nutrients from the mud and water (algae and various microscopic creatures are also quick to colonize these puddles). In fact, they can turn their lives around, from egg to adult to egg, in less than two weeks!

**When eventually the puddle disappears,** every creature dries up and becomes dust too. It sounds harsh, but this is dust with a difference – it's living dust. In the dried-up mud they will have laid eggs and these minuscule capsules of life are able to withstand incredibly hot, dry conditions and so sit it out, waiting for the next downpour – and around they go again!

A hugely magnified triops, which springs back to life once you have nourished it with water and food.

## YOU WILL NEED

> **fine net**
> **plastic container with lid**
> **small pipette or plastic syringe**
> **collection of small jars or test tubes**
> **magnifying lens**

**2** Once you've got home, use a pipette or spoon to sort out the truly tiny creatures from the slightly larger ones. It is the smallest ones that you want to keep for your micro zoo. There wouldn't be much point in calling it a micro zoo otherwise.

**3** Keep your super-small finds in a test tube or a similar lidded container and feed them regularly with green water (see page 21).

**1** Take your fine net out to a pond near you. Try to choose one with good clear water and go hunting on a bright day. All the creatures should be near the surface, making the most of the warmer water. Put your catch in a plastic container with a lid and take it home.

### Take it further

Sometimes you will come across something in your catch that doesn't belong to your micro zoo, but is nevertheless worthy of investigation with a magnifying lens. Here we found a snail egg case on a stick – all the little dots are the newly hatched snails that are crawling around (see also page 35).

# Feed your micro zoo

**The problem with having traditional pets** is that there is not a lot of mystery surrounding their lives. You can buy books on how to keep them, so the challenge simply isn't there. This is where my idea of the perfect pets comes in – the micro zoo that we created on the previous page. They are small, easy to keep and they won't leave unwanted hairs on the sofa. In fact, as they are so small, you can build up a collection of them.

**Look in any puddle** and you will find all manner of tiny dots that, on closer scrutiny, are all part of a huge and complicated miniature eco-system. They are hugely important to the everyday running of any pond, lake, stream or ditch. Understand these little animated dots and you will understand life in the water so much more.

**Your micro zoo animals all feed on microscopic algae and debris** in the water. You can either feed yours with water from where you collected them in the first place or make your own green water (see opposite). There is a fine line between getting the food right and fouling the water. So watch your zoo carefully to make sure that all is well.

**Once you have mastered what these little things need** in their lives to make them happy, you can move onto the 'lions and tigers' of the underwater world – larger insects, such as beetles, water boatmen and dragonfly larvae. But more about them later.

An ostracod is a funny little speck of life. It looks like a tiny full stop but it is quite clearly alive as it whirls around. Look closely and you will see that these crustaceans are contained in a little hard pod of a shell, which they row around with many tiny, hair-like limbs.

## 1

Find a pond that is always full of green water and simply scoop out a jam jar full. Keep the jar in a light position and then you can use the water to feed your micro zoo. Add a little bit on a daily basis.

## 2

If it is the winter and you want a supply of zoo food closer to home, try putting an old lettuce leaf in a jam jar and pouring boiling water on it. Leave the jar in a light and sunny place. Eventually the water will go green. I have also used wheat grains, rice and old banana skins, and all with good results. Your water may smell a little, but that is all part of the process. The 'green' colour is caused by microscopic algae and the little creatures that have colonized it.

### YOU WILL NEED

> jam jar
> pond water or lettuce leaf

## Take it further

* If your water goes green then clear again, what has happened is that you have had a culture of plants that have then fuelled a population of plant-eating creatures, which have consumed everything that was green. Unless you get some more 'green' plants from somewhere, they will die out as quickly as they arrived. So from time to time you may have to add a little green water from another culture or add tiny drops of something called 'liquifry', which you can get at any good pet or aquarium shop.

* Another creature that lives off algae in green water is a small crustacean that is often referred to as cyclops because, just like the mythical Greek monster, it only has one eye spot!

# Ponds and lakes

Here's a thought for you. When does a puddle get so big it becomes a pond? Well, I guess the answer is that a puddle dries up and loses all its water at some time. So a pond could be any body of still water that is always there. But, then, when does a pond become a lake? And what might you find in these masses of water?

**There are many bugs in freshwater habitats**. They can be vegetarian – plant sap-sucking little fellas like the greenfly – or they can be predators feeding on the juices of other creatures. The one thing they have in common is a sharp, dagger-like mouthpart that they use a little like a sharp straw.

**Some of my favourite bugs** are found flipping and skidding across the surface of the water in the summer. These animals include the pond skaters, water crickets (not crickets at all but a shorter, bent-legged pond skater) and water measurers. They live their life on the fragile surface film of the water and they prey on other insects unfortunate enough to get trapped on it.

**Thanks to a few neat inventions,** these animals stay on top and don't sink. They have bent feet that curl up at the ends so they don't pierce the surface tension. (What is surface tension, do I hear you ask? To find out more, turn over the page.) They also have claws further up the leg than you would expect, to stop them punching a hole. Then there is a collection of waterproof hairs that coat the body and legs, giving the animal a greater surface area to spread its weight over.

**These well-developed bugs also use the surface film** to communicate to each other by setting up ripple signals. In a similar way, drowning insects also set up their own ripples of panic. The successful floating bugs are very quick to pick up on these ripples with their sensitive feet and antennae, and before long are on their way to plunder the less fortunate.

Large expanses of weedy water provide security for many birds. Ducks are obvious on most ponds and lakes, as are members of the grebe family, such as this little grebe, or dabchick.

The brown trout is one of the most common of freshwater fish.

This is the larvae of an adult caddis fly. They make a protective home for themselves out of stones, shells or rocks.

The surface tension of water is a death trap to many creatures unable to fight its sticky power. But predatory bugs, such as the pond skater, use it to their advantage.

# So why don't they sink?!

**We have met the pond skater and their relatives** the water measurer and the water cricket, but how do they stay on the right side of the water and not end up sinking? Well I have already described the special water repellent hairs that coat much of their bodies (see page 22), but something even more important is being used and that is something that happens when water meets air. It is called surface tension and acts like a thin skin, so if you are light and can spread your weight over the surface and also tread carefully, you are pretty much doing what a pond skater is doing.

**Here are two quick little demonstrations** that show some more properties of the surface tension – one is my neat little trick (see below) to show how spreading the load helps get surface tension on your side, and the other (see the soap boat, opposite) shows you just how powerful surface tension can be.

**You may well ask, what have either of these got to do with wildlife?** Well the soap boat trick is actually a technique used by the water cricket. So that its prey cannot feel it coming, it goes into stealth mode and simply produces a kind of oily soap from it bottom and silently slides forward.

## Nick's trick

Take a paper clip, which if you were to drop it into a bowl of water, would simply sink – no surprise there, then. But place the clip on a piece of paper and gently push the paper down into the water and the pin should stay where it is, resting on the surface tension. Magic!

# 1
Cut out some small pieces of paper. They can be any shape, but a triangle works well (plus it also looks more like a boat!).

# 2
Shave some pieces of soap off the bar. Use one of the scissor blades, but shave away from you and be very careful.

# 3
Now balance a piece of the shaved soap on one edge of a paper triangle, so that it overhangs. This is your soap boat, which you should gently place on the surface of the bowl of water. Watch what happens – the boat gets pulled along by the surface tension. Behind the boat, the grip of the tension on the boat is weakened and destroyed by the soap. The piece of paper is being pulled forward by the stronger force.

## Take it further

* Catch a water boatman or some other insect that hunts on the water surface and place it in a water tray. Shine a bench lamp on it from above and what do you notice about the shadow that is cast on the bottom of the tray?

* Look at the tips of the feet – why are they not sinking through the water's surface?

# Pond dragons

**Dragonflies and damselflies** are second only to butterflies in their attractive and bright colouring. To tell them apart can be difficult, but on the whole, a dragonfly is larger than the more delicate damselfly.

**The best place to catch up with these brightly coloured examples** of insect life is on a hot, still summer's day by a body of water where they dash, dart, whiz and skip around. Some people are a little scared about getting in so close to these active animals and I guess their wildly inaccurate popular names such as horse stingers, Devil's darning needles or Devil flies don't help! But despite their aggressive attitude to life, the only creatures that should fear these animals are smaller flying ones.

**As a group they are known as the Odonata,** which means 'toothed jaws', and this gives away their game. They really are the winged assassins of the sky, as adults trawling the air for other small insects; even the tiniest of damselflies is a ruthless murderer of midges. So if you wish to get to know dragonflies better, how do you go about it? Well it makes sense to start with the slowest stage of their lives and that means getting to know and study the nymphs: this is what the insects are called at their larval stage. At this time they are much slower beasts, prowling or lying in ambush for smaller prey.

## Fab facts

* Some damselfliess (left) consume up to 20% of their own body weight a day.

* Large dragonflies (far left) can reach speeds of up to 22mph.

Behaviour that is very easy to witness is egg laying, which can be anything from a repeated dipping and dancing flight, spiking the surface of the water with the tip of the abdomen, each time releasing eggs. Others are more careful, settling on vegetation and cautiously positioning the eggs, either gluing or depositing them inside water plants. Some species of damselfly will submerge themselves to get their eggs in a safe place.

But the activity you will notice most will be that of feeding and territory defence as a male dashes this way and that, seeing off impostors and rivals, and not just his own species either. I have seen particularly bold insects have a pop at passing birds.

Mating is easy to see as two insects fly in tandem, with the male towing the female around, held firmly behind the neck with his claspers.

## Take my advice

The avid dragon spotter and damsel watcher needs a few bits of essential equipment.

* A pair of binoculars is very handy, because a lot of the action takes place in the middle of the pond or river.

 * A butterfly net can be useful for getting a closer look, but handling them without hurting them requires skill and patience and is really for those patient and expert at handling insects.

* Buy a good field guide if you want to put names to everything you find (see page 70). A few hours watching these insects is an experience in itself and you can see them doing some amazing things, even if you are not entirely sure what's doing them!

# Hatching dragons

**You can rear your own dragonflies** and watch a very private part of their incredible life cycle. But you first need to collect some dragonfly nymphs, and it's best to choose those from a 'still water' habitat, such as a pond or lake. You are then more likely to be able to provide for the needs of the nymphs from these habitats rather than those from flowing waters.

**You need to find a full-grown or nearly full-grown nymph,** unless you want to spend years feeding it! To spot one of these, look for obviously large examples of dragonfly. Check the wing buds – if they are long, you have more than likely got one in its last nymphal skin. If the nymph is active near the surface of the water, its gills have stopped working. This is a sure-fire clue that it is about to emerge and start to use its adult breahing technique through little holes called spiracles.

## Fab fact

If you find the elongated form of a hawker nymph, you can see nature's original jet engine! The gills of these insects are set inside a cavity in the abdomen, which normally pumps water over it to flush it out. But this action can be turned to a rather surprising piece of predator avoidance as the insect can rapidly squirt the water out backwards, which fires them forwards! You can see this happen if you gently lift one of these insects to the surface of the water; in its agitation it will try to escape. In so doing, it will angle its abdomen tip upwards and you will see it squirt a jet of water up and through the surface.

**1** Set up a fish tank as for any other aquatic life (see page 17) but don't put a lid on it. Setting up the tank outside is best so that if you miss the moment, the insect will at least be free to fly away without bashing itself to pieces indoors. Provide a selection of twigs, branches or reeds in the tank, sticking out of the top for the emerging dragons to climb up.

**2** When you are collecting, you only want two or three large specimens for a fish tank about 50-60cm long. Choose the biggest nymphs you can find as these are likely to turn into adults the most quickly, bearing in mind some of these insects will spend several years in their nymphal stage. If you choose small ones, you may well be in for a long wait! A good tip is to look at the wing buds; they are a good indication of age. Those with longer wings are more likely to hatch during the season. Feed your nymphs on small worms from the garden.

**3** Just before emerging, nymphs tend to hang around near the surface as their gills stop working and they need to start breathing like the adult insect through tiny holes in their thorax called spiracles. It is now that you should keep an eye open for the grand finale! It usually happens in the early morning or evening, so increase your vigil at these times of the day.

**4** If you are lucky, you may see one of the most beautiful sights in the insect world. Following its slow crawl up a stem, the nymph splits open along a weak spot at the back of its head and a new dragonfly is born. If you miss the emergence, be patient and try again.

# Collecting the empty skins

**After a dragonfly has emerged from its nymph stage** and flown away, it leaves its empty skin behind. Search these empty skins and mount as many different ones as possible to make a special collection that you will always enjoy.

**Look around the edges of ponds and streams** in the spring and summer, paying particular attention to any young vegetation. Once you have your eye in you will probably notice dry brown husks that are the old nymphal cases. They are called exuvia and look like perfect hollow nymphs – eyes, jaws and all.

**Most of the empty skins will be stuck to reeds and plant stems** and can be quite a stretch from the safety of the bank. This could prove a bit of a problem to the naturalist wishing to have a closer look. But worry not, this is where a large yogurt pot and bamboo cane become invaluable – see opposite.

## Nick's trick

* Nymphs are totally concerned with feeding and although they may look sluggish and clumsy, they have a secret weapon – a set of extendible jaws – one of the most complex hunting gadgets in existence.

* This deadly device is hinged under the head and when the nymph sees potential dinner (a passing tadpole, fish or other nymph), it extends its arm-like lip and stabs, grabs or spears the prey so fast that the action cannot be followed with the naked eye.

* If you catch a nymph case, soak it in water to make it less brittle and then use a needle or pin to tease out that extendible jaw that was once every worm and tadpole's worst nightmare!

> **large yogurt pot**
> **bamboo cane**
> **scissors**
> **gaffer tape**
> **cardboard**
> **glue**

**1** Securely attach the bamboo cane to the bottom of the pot with a few strips of gaffer tape.

**2** You now have the perfect device for reaching out over boggy, marshy ground or deep water to where these dry remnants of dragonfly life are often positioned.

**3** Scrape the edge of the pot upwards and the old skin should drop into it. This can get a little tricky in windy weather!

**4** If the skins aren't fresh, they can get a bit crispy, but if you are careful, you can glue or pin them to a bit of cardboard and then try to identify the different types. In this picture, a pair of damselflies are on the left and two dragonflies are on the right.

# Pond snails

**There are several kinds of mollusc that inhabit freshwater**. First there are filter-feeding ones that live between half shells. These are members of the clam family, and trawling around in the mud or gravel may reveal several species, from tiny little freshwater cockles to the giant swan mussel, which is at least 20cm long.

**In weedy freshwater you will also find true snails**. There are many different kinds that inhabit the underwater world. Collect some weed or some mud from the bottom and you will almost certainly find a few of these molluscs slowly creeping about. You know you have a snail because it usually has a shell with some kind of twist to it and it moves by gliding around on a big muscular foot.

**You can further divide these** into those that breathe air and have a breathing hole or pore that opens into a simple lung and those that only breathe through their skin. These also often have a 'door' called an operculum, which they can pull into the shell entrance, giving further protection to the snail.

**Watch the snails you have collected** and if some of them are active and start 'walking' upside down, hanging from the water's surface, you may notice them opening their breathing hole. Snails that will best show this are also some of the most common and largest you will come across, like the great pond snail and the ramshorn.

## Fab facts

The snail's breathing hole leads to a chamber called the mantle cavity, which is used a bit like a lazy lung. Air wafts in and all the oxygen the snail wants is picked up by a network of blood vessels in the skin. Keep some great pond snails in a jam jar next to your bed at night and you can actually hear breathing, a kind of popping noise as they come to the surface and open their breathing pore. Some water snails have gills and fill their mantle cavity with water, extracting oxygen from it, while others have a combination of both.

**1** Write the letters 'A' and 'B' on two of the sticky labels. Stick the labels to the jam jars.

**2** Fill jam jar 'A' with normal water from the tap. For the water in jam jar 'B' you need to remove most of the dissolved oxygen. Do this by boiling water and allowing it to cool to the same temperature as the other. Pour it into jar 'B'.

**3** Place a snail of about the same size in each jar. Use the stop watch to see how long each snail spends at the surface with its breathing pore open. Also count how many times this happens during that length of time.

**4** The snail in oxygen-poor water, jar 'B', needs to breath at the surface more than the snail in jar 'A'. It cannot get as much oxygen from the water as it needs.

## Take it further

All snails can breath to an extent through their skin as well as through their breathing pore (see Fab facts, opposite). This experiment proves that pond snails use both methods of breathing. When the dissolved oxygen level is deliberately reduced, the breathing pore comes into use more frequently.

# Food file

**Most pond snails graze plants stems and the water's surface**, rasping away a layer of cells or microscopic algae as they go. You can watch pond snails as they cling to the underside of the water surface and graze the film of microscopic plants; or pop one in a jam jar and watch it slide up the side of the glass. If it is feeding, you will see its radula move backwards and forwards almost like a jaw. Look through a magnifying glass and you may even see some of the hundreds of tiny teeth that give the radula a rough, file-like surface, perfect for the job.

**Here is a pond snail hard at work chomping its way through a particularly delicious plant stem.**

## Nick's trick

* Why not collect any empty shells you find? It is common to collect shells on the beach, but how many people do you know that collect freshwater mollusc shells? They are just as interesting and are less studied than their salt water cousins.

* Simply wash them in warm, soapy water, dry them on a tea towel and rub with some baby oil or similar to make them shiny. Then try to identify what you have collected using a good field guide. Add a label to each specimen with time, date, location and a little habitat information, such as whether the water was hard or soft, clear or dirty, still or flowing, and slowly you will get to know this little-studied but fascinating bunch of water residents.

**1** If you keep an observation tank or look closely at the stems of plants and particularly under the flat leaves of lily pads, you may find small, slimy blobs of clear jelly.

**2** Depending on how old they are, you may notice up to several hundred tiny 'pips' inside. These blobs are snail egg clusters and the little dots are the individual developing embryos; the baby snails.

**3** Different snails each lay slightly different egg masses, some are rounded, and others are crescent shaped and some look like little clear sausages.

## Take it further

* If you collect a plant with one of these egg clusters on it and place it in a shallow dish of pond water, you can keep a snail diary. Look at them each day and keep a record and even draw their development. How long do they take to hatch?

* Once they hatch, you can release the snails back where you got them or you could rear them as part of your micro zoo (see page 18).

* Experiment with the types of food you offer them. Try pond weed or lettuce leaves and make sure you keep the water clean and fresh. As they grow, have a guess at what species they are.

# A most exciting hole

**If you have the space,** do yourself and all your local wildlife a favour – build yourself a pond! Any permanent water acts as a wildlife magnet, not just for the things that live in water but for other creatures that hunt around its edges or simply visit to drink or have a scrub up.

**There are many ways you can turn a scruffy garden corner** or dull expanse of lawn into a pond, but it does depend a little on your budget and skills. The easiest way is to buy a pre-moulded pond from a garden centre. However, they tend to be a bit steep sided and also you are restricted to someone else's design and so finding one to fit your imagination can be difficult.

**The alternative is to get some plastic sheeting,** but not any old plastic. Cheap plastic eventually becomes brittle and then just a badly placed rock or even the claws of an animal is all it takes to turn a watery oasis into a dry hole in the ground, full of dead and dying pond life. The best material to line your pond with is butyl rubber. This is thick, flexible and guaranteed for 20–25 years. Furthermore, you can get it from a good garden centre off the roll.

**Before you start digging,** draw a plan of what your pond will look like, how deep it will be and where you will plant things. Think about how wildlife will use it too. Some of the ideas you might like to incorporate into your design could be a deep bit that stays free of ice in the winter; somewhere shallow where birds can bathe and where frogs and other creatures can easily get in and out of the water; and you might want to plant some emergent plants, such as reeds or rushes, for dragonflies and other insects to rest up on.

**YOU WILL NEED**

> **spade**
> **fine sand**
> **old newspapers**
> **old carpets, matting or rugs**
> **pond liner made of butyl rubber**

# 1
Dig a hole to match your plan – the centre needs to be at least 50cm deep to prevent a total freeze-up in winter. Keep it reasonably shallow around the edge for plants. This is hard work on your own, even if you are only planning on a small one. I find a bit of bribery works well on family, friends and relatives, such as a good barbecue once you've finished.

# 2
Get into your pond on all fours and investigate the ground very carefully to ensure you remove anything that is sharp or hard and might puncture your pond liner. Put down a 5cm thick layer of sand and then, if you have any newspapers, old carpets, matting or rugs, put them on top of this. Only now is it safe to put down your pond liner.

# 3
Gently mould the liner into the shape of your pond, carefully folding it into corners and obstacles. Bury any liner remaining at the edges in a small trench or weigh down with stones or soil.

# 4
Now it is time for the most satisfying job of all – sitting back and letting the hosepipe do the work, filling your pond with water. Leave the water to stand for a few days to allow the chlorine to evaporate before introducing plants and any pond life.

## Take my advice

* You need to buy enough pond liner to cover the area of your pond plus enough to cover the sides and the ledges and any irregularity in the surface.

* The formula is to take the longest distance across the pond and add to this the maximum depth of the pond times two. Then add 50cm. This will give you the length of pond liner you need to buy.

# Frog watch

**The life cycle of a frog or toad** is tied to water, so they need to live in damp and dank places. This, of course, means they are hard to find. For most of the year they wander about, some lurking near the pond, others going walkies, and newts in particular can get into surprising places. I've even found them up trees!

**All amphibians need their surroundings to be relatively moist,** so the best time to look for them is at night, when they're at their most active. It's also the time when most of their food is on the move. Go out with a torch – a head torch is preferable as it leaves your hands free – and scour your flowerbeds, log piles and lawns and you may well turn up a hunting frog or toad.

**The best and probably most exciting time** to look for frogs and toads is during the breeding season, when they return to water to lay their eggs. At this time their activities are also a little more predictable. In spring, when the temperature is around 8°C, visit you local pond or lake after dark and investigate the edges for amphibian life.

**Ripples and sounds tend to give away the locations of frogs and toads;** even if they are fleeing, you will hear a loud 'plop' as they leap to the safety of the water. Be patient and you will eventually catch sight of them, either swimming below the surface or returning to the top to breathe.

## Fab facts

\* Listen out for the different sounds frogs and toads make when the males are calling to the females. Frogs tend to purr like quiet little motors, while it is toads that make the famous 'croak'.

\* If you find spawn that occurs in long strings, then you have found the spawn of toads, who generally prefer deeper water to common frogs. But with shallow edges and deep centres to most ponds, it can be quite confusing as both species take part in their mass spawning in the same water.

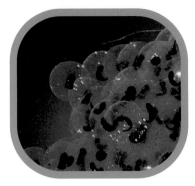

**1** The best place to look for amphibian spawn is still water with lots of plant life. The bubbly masses of frogspawn are familiar to most of us. Freshly laid spawn is quite firm and tightly squashed together, which means it is only hours old and the frogs will not be far away. As soon as it is laid, the protective jelly coating starts to soak up the surrounding water and swell.

**2** When the frogspawn hatches, tiny tadpoles are born. For the first few days of their lives they hardly move. They have no mouths yet and they are surviving by absorbing their yolk sac.

**3** After about six weeks, their back legs start to grow and their appetite starts to grow too. By the time their front legs are growing, the amphibian diet becomes much more meat based.

**4** And so the tadpole slowly turns into a frog, shedding its tail on the way. It has plenty to celebrate!

# From 'pole to froglet

**Every year and hopefully for ever more,** young people will peer into a pond and get excited at the first sight of the jellied mass shimmering right there. The next instinct is to unceremoniously stuff the spawn into a bucket and take it home. Sadly, these well-meaning acts of curiosity often end in disaster. Many tadpoles perish and few make it to froghood.

**There are many simple reasons for this,** so here is my fool-proof, frog-rearing recipe! Remember that the more tadpoles you have, the more work you will have to do to keep the water fresh. They take more feeding, more cleaning out and they may even have detrimental effects on each other by slowing down development or becoming cannibalistic. The end result is many deaths and a higher percentage of failure.

**Collect spawn from garden ponds wherever possible.** It keeps your disturbance of wild populations to a minimum. Get it from just one place, too, to avoid spreading certain frog diseases. Once you have successfully bred your tadpoles, the husbandry becomes very labour intensive, so it is best now to release your froglets back to the area where you collected the spawn. Do this after dark and into long vegetation, not back into the water.

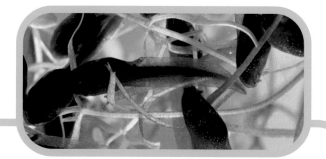

## Nick's tricks

Feeding hungry tadpoles can be hard work. Here are some ideas for you. Try to get a balance and do not overfeed or you will have to increase the number of water changes.

* When they need to eat meat, feed them flaked fish foods and small pond creatures, such as blood worms and daphnia, also called water fleas, which you can buy from any fish or pet shop. Also feed them very small hatchling crickets, aphids and other tiny terrestrial insects.

* Every few days, feed them dry pellets usually intended for herbivorous pets such as rabbits. Another bit of variety is lettuce boiled for 5 minutes. Put on the surface, a leaf at a time.

**1** Choose a medium-sized tank with a vented and well-fitting lid. Always use rain or other natural water. Tap water can be used but let it stand for a couple of days so the chlorine naturally disappears. Washed gravel and pond plants will help the water quality and also provide food for hungry taddies. Set the 'tadpolery' in a light location but out of direct sunlight.

**2** Collect a small quantity of newly laid fresh spawn, which, when only a couple of days old, is quite firm and easy to separate with your fingers into a manageable portion. A half cupful is perfect to achieve a ratio of three to five tadpoles for every litre of water.

**3** Acclimatize your catch to the water in your tank. Put the spawn in a plastic bag and float on the surface for two hours. Then gently mix the tank water with that in the bag and tip in the spawn. For a few days the tadpoles hardly move. Do not disturb! Once they start swimming, change half the water (see left).

## Take my advice

To change the water, each week tip half the water through a net or sieve so you catch any stray tadpoles. Pop them back in the tank. Replace the water with fresh, non-chlorinated water of a similar temperature. If the water gets cloudy, make the changes more frequently or add a couple of other herbivores, such as a few pond snails, to do some cleaning for you.

**4** For the first couple of weeks your tadpoles will be content micro-grazing algae off the sides of the tank and any vegetation. But after three weeks they start needing larger quantities of more substantial salad (see Nick's tricks, opposite).

**5** As the tadpoles grow, increase their food. Then, with the arrival of front legs, reduce the water level to a few centimetres. Give them places to climb to, such as moss and stones, and soon you will have froglets. Congratulations!

# Bubbles of life

**If you have ever kept fish,** you will know that it is a good idea to put some water plants or pond weed in the tank with them. But have you ever wondered why? Well a clue can be seen if you visit a shallow pond on a warm, sunny day.

**Look closely at the submerged plants** and you will notice that not only are the leaves covered with what looks like millions of little silver baubles, but also there is a stream of bubbles fizzing to the surface. What is this gas? To answer this question there is a very simple little demonstration that you can do (see opposite).

**Your pond plant has produces oxygen** (and all plants, not just pond weed produce it) as a result of photosynthesis. This in itself is handy as all life on earth needs this gas to survive. It is why plants are good for fish and for water life in general as they produce oxygen, some of which dissolves in the water and, in turn, is breathed through the gills of many aquatic creatures.

This is probably one of my favourite pond insects. The great diving beetle is a top-notch predator. Both the adult and the larvae, which are known as 'water tigers', are enthusiastic predators of tadpoles, fish and any other small pond animal they can overpower.

## YOU WILL NEED

> **jar**
> **pond weed (Canadian pond weed works well)**
> **plastic funnel**
> **test tube**
> **desk lamp or sunny window sill**
> **taper**
> **matches**

**1** Fill the jar with water and then put in the pond weed.

**2** Put the jar in the fish tank filled with water and cover it with the plastic funnel. This main part of the funnel has to be entirely submerged and the weed must sit underneath.

**3** Then take the test tube, fill it with water in the fish tank and place over the neck of the funnel. It is important that the tube remains full of water as you put it over the funnel.

**4** Place the whole set-up in a bright, sunny place, such as on a window sill or next to a table lamp, and wait and watch.

**5** Little bubbles will start to form on the leaves and slowly these will stream upwards, collecting in the top of the tube.

**6** One of the tests for oxygen is to light a wooden splint and then blow it out so that it still glows. Quickly remove the test tube from the tank, pour out the water and then push the taper into the tube. If the splint bursts back into flame, you have oxygen.

# Feed the ducks

**This book is really too small** to go into all the different and fascinating kinds of bird behaviour you can see in and around water and wetlands but, having said that, there are a few pointers that can enliven the most mudane visit to the duck pond or throw a whole new perspective on the way you look at wild waterfowl and waders.

**Just a simple trip to the local duck pond** can give you much more than the sight of a dozen greedy mallards stuffing their beaks! It can be a brilliant way to start looking at the world through different eyes. Before you go, take some breadcrumbs and rice and soak half in water. Then, on arrival at the pond, feed a mixture of floating and sinking food to the ducks. Notice the different ways the birds eat the food (see opposite).

## Take my advice

* Many freshwater birds dive, but some are better at it than others. It is mainly used for two reasons: to avoid predators and to give the birds access to food. Next time you notice a bird diving, try to time how long it spends underwater and guess at what it is doing while down there.

* Different birds have different diving techniques too. Those born to swim, like the tufted duck, pochard and grebe, dive by giving a little upward jump before slipping below the surface, without too much of a splash. Others, such as mallards, will usually make a real meal of trying to submerge.

**1** The food floating on the surface, especially if it is ground up fine, is skimmed off the water with a snaffling action. This is a technique called 'dabbling' and is why ducks like mallards are called dabbling ducks! It is also the reason that ducks have that characteristic wide bill.

**2** When the same ducks come to deal with the sinking food, well that is a different matter. This is when they have to make a little more effort and it is quite common to see ducks like mallards up-ending with their bottoms in the air, to give them a greater reach to the pond's bottom to get the food. A mallard can reach down by up to 45cm!

**3** Now you have seen this behaviour look around to see what other feeding techniques are being used. Many use variations on the dabbling theme, but because they have different body and neck lengths they can reach different depths, which means they can all live together without eating each other's food and getting in the way. Just watch swans, for example, they can get down to depths of about a metre. Other ducks like pochard and tufted ducks dive for their food. Some birds like coot and moorhen are not ducks and do not even have totally webbed feet, they pick at their food and they dive too.

*Take it further*

* Look closely at a duck's bill (binoculars might be helpful for this) and you should be able to see how it works. By pumping their bristly tongues backwards and forwards in the beak, water is sucked in at the tip and squirted out through the sides.

* Look closer still and you will see the duck's filter, which shows up as a row of tiny little ridges or serrations, a little bit like a comb. In the same way you can take a mouthful of noodle soup and squirt the liquid from between your teeth keeping the noodles in your mouth, a duck filters small creatures, algae and even your breadcrumbs. (Incidentally, when trying the trick with the soup, do not tell your parents where you learnt your bad table manners!)

# Rivers and streams

Whether it is water in the sky, a pond or a puddle, it is always going somewhere. Water moves. That is what it does – even water in our own body cells merely borrows it and off it goes again. This continuous motion is, of course, known as the water cycle (see also page 4).

**It is in our rivers and streams that the mass movement of water** is at its most obvious. These are the places where water has collected in the creases and seams of the landscape and once collected in them, it finds the fastest and most direct route downwards. It is pushed by gravity towards our oceans, which are continually refilled at their source by rain, snow and other forms of precipitation (that's the posh word for any water in any form that falls out of the sky!).

**The difference between a river and a stream** is that a river is basically the final thing. It is the biggest form of flowing water and always flows into the sea. Every other body of flowing water is smaller and flows into a river. But now it is time to find out more about what lives in and around them.

**Where you have flowing water**, you have a very different selection of creatures to those you would usually find in still water. One of the major differences in fast-flowing water is that many insects have a flatter shape to help them stay where they want to be, rather than be carried away by the current.

**Oxygen levels in the water** also play an important part in what lives where. The upper stretches of rivers and streams are important nursery grounds for many fish, such as salmon and trout, who can travel many thousands of miles to lay their eggs here. In the slower-moving water, there is less mixing and bubbling of air and water and so a different community of creatures that need less oxygen will be found here.

A sign of healthy, clean water is that a young brown trout will spend much of its time sitting out of the current behind a rock, making dashes for food as it gets swept past.

Water voles are found where water is flowing so slowly, it is practically stationary. They will visit nearby ponds, too.

A kingfisher is a frustrating bird to watch as it is easily disturbed and fast flying. Listen out for its distinctive piping call and learn to spot the electric-blue comet as it zings past.

When your river is healthy, it can support top predators, such as otters.

# Kick sampling

**Gaze into the fast riffles and frothing rapids** and it may seem an impossible place for life to hang on, but it does and it is there. But, if you were an insect living in fast-flowing water, you would try to spend as little time as possible in the open water. Not only are you exposed to predators, but you are also at risk of being swept away and pummelled to a pulp. So any creatures living here are to be found in the shelter of weed beds or among pebbles, boulders or sediment on the stream bottom.

**Here is the catch though** – try to use a net in the traditional way and, at best, you will end up with a net bag full of gravel, grit or boulders. At worst you will simply bust your net! So let the vigorous current do the hard work for you.

**This technique is called kick sampling** and it is one method that biological scientists use to find out which creatures live in our rivers and streams. This is useful knowledge, because by looking at who lives in the water, we can find out how clean it is.

## Watch out!

Very fast water is a force to be reckoned with. It carves the hardest rocks as if they are butter and literally shapes our landscapes forever. With this in mind, it is important that you respect this power when you are exploring in or around it. One mistake or false move could end up with you being swept off down stream. So, for safety's sake, practise kick sampling in quieter water, albeit water with a fairly brisk flow, otherwise it simply doesn't work.

**1** Hold your net in one hand, downstream from where you wish to investigate. Allow the current to unfurl and fill your net.

**2** Then, either using your feet or a stout stick, kick around in the sediment immediately upstream from your waiting net. Any heavy sediment will settle before it gets to your net, but any delicate creatures that had been clinging for dear life among the boulders will be swept up and the current will take them into your net. They will then be held there by the current until you lift the net out to investigate your catch. This works just as well if you shake up weed and other potential homes for small creatures.

## Take it further

* When using this technique, try sampling different areas of the stream. Look at what creatures live in the silt and sediment and compare this with those that live in the faster water.

* Do different animals live among boulders, weed or gravel? Look at their different adaptations to life in each habitat.

# Make a light trap

We have all heard of the old saying, 'Like a moth to a flame', right? Well, it's not just moths that are mysteriously attracted to light at night. All manner of creatures for some unknown reason will flock to an artificial light source.

So, one of the ways underwater life can be trapped is by making use of this, by combining light with a trap (see opposite).

Different habitats at different times of the year can reveal different creatures. So do not be too disheartened if you do not catch much, simply make a note of this and try somewhere else. If you are using your light trap in a current, make sure the funnel entrance is pointing downstream.

The sorts of creatures you might catch depends on what you have in your river. But you can at least expect a selection of crustaceans, such as freshwater shrimps and their relatives, and you might get a crayfish or even an eel or two.

Once you have finished making your trap, take it to your favourite stream at dusk, lower it into the water and then return in the morning to see what you have caught.

**2** Cover one end of the drainpipe with some of the black plastic, securing it with plenty of gaffer tape.

**3** Take your waterproof torch, make sure you have changed the batteries to give you the longest trapping time, turn it on and tape it inside your trap, facing towards the entrance.

**1** Take your empty drinks bottle and cut off the top, about 10cm down.

**4** Slide the stones into the bottom of the drainpipe to weight it once the trap is in the water.

**5** Insert the cut-off top of the drinks bottle into the drainpipe with the pouring end facing into the drainpipe.

**6** Using more pieces of gaffer tape, secure the top of the drinks bottle in place. Now you're ready to go fishing.

# Mud tracking

**Wherever water and soil meet**, you get soft stuff: mud, sand and silt. This means that while you are exploring near water you may well come across footprints left by any manner of creatures that have visited the stream to fish, drink, hunt, wash or cross over it.

**Soft but firm mud is the best** and you will probably have good conditions by rivers after the water level has fallen following a period of wet weather. Look out for the spidery tracks of rats, mice and voles, and if you are lucky, you may find those left by an otter. There will be many tracks left by water birds, too, simply visiting for a wash and a drink.

**You can keep this evidence very easily** using the old naturalist's technique of making a plaster cast of the footprints. Not only can you keep them and collect them, you can have some fun trying to identify them too!

**I have gathered a huge collection of prints from around the world** in exactly this way, most found next to rivers, ponds and in old dried-up puddles. The fun really comes in knowing that you have a little bit of evidence that is not only unique to a species but to the individual animal that made it. You have made the first steps towards becoming a tracker and with the help of a book of animal tracks and signs (see page 70), you should be able to identify your footprint.

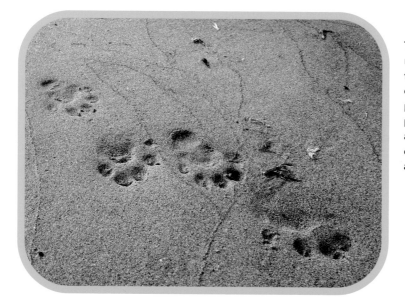

The edge of ponds, streams and rivers, especially those whose levels fluctuate, are good places for a bit of tracking. Soft mud makes for a perfect footprint. Expect to find the prints of many different mammals and birds. If you are lucky, you may even find a trail, like this one left by an otter.

- > **large plastic drinks bottle with the top cut off and then a 2.5cm wide strip of the plastic**
- > **paper clip**
- > **bag of plaster of Paris**
- > **water**
- > **stick**
- > **pinch of salt**
- > **paint**
- > **paintbrush**

**1** Clear any debris carefully away from your chosen footprint and make sure the mud or sand is firm and not too watery. (This is easily tested by gently pressing your finger into the ground and taking it out again. If the hole remains, it is okay.)

**2** Take the strip of plastic and make a ring that will easily encircle the footprint. Fasten it in place with the paper clip. An alternative method, if the mud is dry and thick enough, is to make a small bank of soil around the footprint. This works in exactly the same way, damming the runny plaster and keeping it in the right place.

**3** Put some of plaster of Paris in the bottom part of the plastic drinks bottle. Then slowly add water, stirring constantly to remove lumps. You want the plaster to be runny enough to drip heavily off your stirrer without sticking, but not too watery.

**4** As soon as you have the consistency right, add a pinch of salt and pour the plaster steadily into your mould. Give the cast a few taps to release any bubbles that may be lurking. Leave for 15 minutes for the plaster to set. Then gently pick up the cast, print and all, wrap well and take it home.

**5** When at home, leave for two days to set hard. Then use a soft brush to wipe away any fragment of mud. You can now paint it. You can make your plaster cast a little less likely to flake and break by painting it with PVA glue, which sets clear.

# Sticklebacks

**It is the original 'tiddler'**, but the three-spined stickleback is more than just small fry. This plucky little fish is probably one of the most successful and adaptable creatures you are likely to meet in a river and, for that matter, in just about any kind of water from the ocean, through streams and ditches to ponds. In fact, any body of permanent water can be home to these tough little tiddlers.

**Once you have caught some** and are looking at them through the sides of a clear vessel, they are instantly recognizable as they have a set of three spines along the top of their backs. In the spring, the male's throat and belly blush a bright red and his eyes become sky blue, while the duller greenish female swells as her belly becomes ripe with eggs. This is when life in your local stickleback community gets really interesting.

**At this time of year, the males become ferocious,** scarlet little warriors defending a territory against any intruders unless, of course, they are adult females. If a female stickleback should enter the scene, a male starts trying to impress, showing off with an energetic zigzag dance. If she shows interest, he will try to lead his lady down to a nest he has made in the weed. It doesn't look like much to us – just a short tunnel in the weed at the bottom of the river – but, for a fish, this nest is a masterpiece of engineering.

**You can set up a freshwater aquarium in the spring** and watch all this for yourself in the comfort of your home. The stickleback makes an excellent little pet and really interesting subject (see opposite).

## Take my advice

Remember that once you have finished studying your sticklebacks you should put them back in the water where you originally got them from.

> **fish tank set up as
>    on page 17**
> **fishing net**

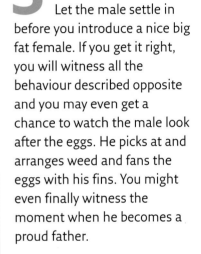

**2** Go fishing!

**3** Let the male settle in before you introduce a nice big fat female. If you get it right, you will witness all the behaviour described opposite and you may even get a chance to watch the male look after the eggs. He picks at and arranges weed and fans the eggs with his fins. You might even finally witness the moment when he becomes a proud father.

**1** Set up your fish tank with clean water, plenty of insect food and some weed and mud at the bottom for the male to make a nest in. The trick is to get the tank set up and settled for a week or so before you go looking for a bright male.

## Take it further

* Pop a small shaving mirror on the end of a stick (or just use your hands) and show your catch his own reflection. What you will see is terrifying territorial behaviour as he puffs himself up, flares his gills and bites at his false foe!

* Carry out other experiments to see just what it is that pushes his buttons. Is it size? Shape? Or colour? As a test, make life-size models from modelling clay and paint some red, some any other colour. Try fish and non-fish shapes and see what he reacts to.

# Water wings

**It seems that birds are attracted to water** like iron filings to a magnet. Wherever there is water they can be found, and usually they are doing interesting things. You just need to put a shallow dish of water out on your garden lawn and sooner or later a bird will be using it as a bath or simply having a convenient drink of fresh water.

**In upland, fast-flowing waters, you may well see a cool little bird** that I like to think of as the James Bond of the bird world – the dipper. Here's a dapper little brown chap with a neat white bib. He's not especially remarkable looking, but he does lead the most extraordinary daredevil existence. The dipper is a bird that favours the fastest riffles. Spot one and stick with it and sooner or later it will plunge headfirst and disappear in the foam, only to return to the surface for a breath or to dispatch a lively water insect or to remove a caddis larva from its case on a convenient nearby rock.

**Early on in the year, the dipper is rather territorial** and because their territories simply run up and down the length of their patch of river you can very easily work out where it begins and ends. Mapping your local birds' territories is interesting and is a really good way of getting to know how they like to operate.

## Fab facts

* You will never forget seeing your first dipper. They truly have a remarkable way of life.

* What you can't see is that as soon as the bird has plunged below the surface it uses its wings to fly under water.

* It also has a set of clear protective eyelids that act a little like underwater goggles!

* Even better – using its heavily clawed feet, it hangs onto the rocks at the bottom while searching for aquatic insects.

**1** As you walk along the edge of the river bank, the bird will fly ahead of you in one direction or the other. Simply follow it. Every time it sees you, it will move on and once you get to the point where the bird turns around and flies back the way it came, you have reached the territory edge!

**2** Make a mark on your map and go back the other way, and repeat until you find the other limit. On the way you can also mark on your map the various perch rocks and any bridges and walls that are overhanging the water, as these are likely places for the bird to nest. Very soon you will have a good idea of the way your local dippers use their bit of river, how they divide it between them, where the stones the males sing from are – even their nest site.

## Take it further

Many water birds have territories that you can work out in this way. The dipper is the easiest, but try seeing if you can piece together the territories of a kingfisher or wagtail. It's easiest to do this in the breeding season as the birds' lives revolve around the nest site.

# Otter spotter

**To see an otter in the wild you need oodles of good luck.** Come to think of it, seeing any mammal that either lives in or visits water is a rare occasion. But wildlife does have an extraordinary way of sneaking up and surprising you, so start trying to spot an otter now, and who knows what will happen.

**Even if you don't get to see one immediately,** just to know they are in the area is, without a shadow of doubt, a wonderful thing. This is where you have to put on your detective hat and become a wildlife equivalent of Sherlock Holmes.

**For most of the time,** the closest you can actually get to a mammal like an otter is by signs of their passing, in this case quite literally – I'm talking poo. The correct word for otter poo is, in fact, spraint, and if you want to be taken seriously in the naturalist's world, it's worth remembering this.

**To the nose of a fellow otter,** a spraint tells them an awful lot of information about who else is about. This, of course, isn't so easy for us humans, but at the most basic level, a spraint does at least tell us that otters are in the area and how recently.

**A spraint can contain feathers of water birds, fur and frog bones, but in most cases it is a rare spraint that doesn't contain fish bones and scales.**

## Take my advice

* When you are looking for an otter spraint, remember that although the otter is the size of a small dog, its spraint is not of the size you might expect from the canine equivalent. So don't look for something that's too big! Yes, they can be tiny little blobs less than a centimetre long, but equally they can be up to 8cm long. They are greenish to black in colour and contain remains of what the otter has eaten, which is always valuable information to a naturalist.

* To confirm it is definitely an otter, smell it! But don't get your nose too close. Getting any dung near your nose is a bad thing and can be dangerous. But, perhaps surprisingly, an otter spraint smells quite pleasant – if it was a mink's spraint, it would probably have you retching in seconds!

Otters leave spraints in places where other otters will stumble upon them and get an update on who is where and how long ago. The sorts of places that are favoured as scent posts are landmarks, such as a rock or a tree root. The rule I find works well is if it seems obvious to you, then the chances are it will stand out to an otter too.

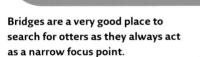

Bridges are a very good place to search for otters as they always act as a narrow focus point.

## Nick's trick

While scurrying around on the river bank, do not forget that most obvious of field signs – the footprint. Check all the soft spots, sandy beaches and muddy hollows as all can act as a natural etch-a-sketch, giving you further clues to what's about. Footprints can confirm your hunches and also let you know what other regular visitors the river is getting. Try taking a plaster cast (see page 53).

# The 'jilly' jar

**Catching fish is surely a most pleasurable and relaxing pastime.** Sitting or standing still and waiting for something to happen is an activity that is rare enough in our fast-paced world. Waiting and stalking and being quiet are also great skills for a naturalist to develop. I have had badgers run into me, otters swim by and even watched a stoat steal eggs from a swan's nest – and all while I have been sitting on a river bank with the string from my jilly jar in hand.

**But what's a jilly jar?** Well, look opposite and you will see. A net is easy to wield and you may think yourself a bit of a hot shot with one, but try catching fast, open-water fish like minnows and sticklebacks with one and you will soon realize it is next to impossible.

## Nick's tricks

* One way of observing fish is obviously in a fish tank (see page 17), but when it comes to seeing them in the wild, it gets a bit more difficult. If the water is clear, then we can see into it, but it can be difficult to see beyond the ripples and waves and light that bounces about all over the place.

* This is where an underwater viewer comes in handy. Get hold of an empty ice-cream tub with a close-fitting lid. Cut the bottom out of the tub and the centre out of the lid, leaving the edge with the seal to act as a frame. Cover the sides of the tub with dark waterproof paint or gaffer tape to eliminate glare. Then stretch cling film over the top of the tub and put on the lid to fasten it in place. Turn the tub upside down, put the cling film against the surface of the water and start viewing.

## 1

Take your jar and tie a piece of string around it really tight so that it doesn't slip off. Then tie a support brace around the bottom of the jar for extra security and make a handle.

## 2

Put small pieces of bread in the jar to act as bait. You can simply soak some in water in the jar and hope it stays in place against the flow of water or the escape of air bubbles from the trap. Alternatively, make a deluxe trap by gluing a little net bag to the bottom of your jar and fill this with the bait.

## 3

Lower your jar into shallow water where you can see lots of small fish activity and wait. Curious fish will start to assemble around the jar, bumping into it from all angles and then pretty soon they will find their way to the mouth of the jar and enter.

## 4

Hoist the jar, water, fish and all, as quickly as you can to the surface. Once you have observed your catch, return it to where it came from.

### Take my advice

The size of jar that you use doesn't really matter although a bigger jar doesn't necessarily catch more fish. Also, the extra weight of water it has to support when you pull it out might break the string.

# Boggy, soggy bits

Easily overlooked – bogs, soaks, swamps, marshes, mires or morasses (call them what you like) – these moist, spongy corners of the countryside are some of the most exquisite jewels. Sadly, they are becoming rarer as the countryside is progressively drained and 'improved' to increase the amount of livestock and crops that can be squeezed onto it.

**Marshes and wetlands** come about in many different ways:

> They can be formed by springs.
> An impermeable bedrock may come close to the surface and so the water is held in place like a bowl.
> They can be slow-moving streams that have divided or got clogged up.
> Or they can be around the edges of existing water and so be a kind of overspill.

**However they are formed,** to spot one you need to look out for dips and gullies in the landscape. Imagine how water moves downhill and collects into pools and puddles, which are the places where bogs form.

**As unattractive as the name bog sounds,** these places can be surprisingly colourful. In acidic bogs, in particular, the habitat supports large numbers of a relatively few species and they put on big spectacles. The mass flowering of bog asphodel or the seeding of hundreds of heads of cotton grass rival any spring woodland.

**Even little carnivorous plants such as sundew,** with their red leaves and stems, and bog mosses, in yellow, red, orange and bright green, can put on vibrant colour displays. As for the larger creatures, look out for breeding wading birds, dragonflies and the hobby, a bird of prey that loves to munch dragonflies and other insects on the wing.

Cotton grass seed heads bob about in the breeze. They love very wet soil conditions so their presence usually means deep water. Avoid walking where these plants grow.

Bog asphodel in the late summer, when the flower stems turn a firey red and yellow.

A golden plover looking very content in its boggy patch of ground.

Bogs are more than a squelchy inconvenience that you might get your wellie boot stuck in. They are a rich and specialized habitat that is all too rare nowadays.

## Watch out!

If you have a boggy bit nearby, obviously be careful, as sometimes these places have deep water that looks nothing more than a patch of wet grassland, and there are few enough naturalists as it is without losing more in the mire! Seriously though, tread carefully, not only for the sake of the creatures and plants that live there, but also for your own safety.

# Beastly botanicals

**Regular plants get their food by a process called photosynthesis,** which literally translated means 'putting together with light'. Deep within their leaves they combine water and carbon dioxide and, using energy harnessed from the Sun, build sugars. But all plants also need other nutrients to survive. These minerals are in the compost, and a plant absorbs them from the soil with its roots. Among the most important of these elements are nitrates and phosphates.

**The problem with the water-logged soil of bogs** is that there isn't much in the way of nutrients. It is either washed away or simply never produced in enough quantities in the first place. In the wet, oxygen-deficient soil, the bacteria and microbes that break down dead material in normal soil simply do not survive in any numbers. So any plant that can develop an alternative is going to have a head start on the competitors. As a result, in bogs, plant families have gone for being carnivorous.

**Plants are experts at attracting insects.** They do it all the time by using flowers, but carnivorous plants have gone one step further. They attract insects, trap them and then digest them and so get their ration of fertilizer from their bodies.

**The most common types found are the sundews and butterworts.** Both have modified leaves that act as sticky traps – a bit like fly paper. Their leaves are covered in glandular hairs.

## Take my advice

Carnivorous plants grow in bogs and damp areas in acidic habitats, such as heathland and moor. If you find some, why not get down on your hands and knees and record the different insects that you find stuck to the leaves? A magnifying glass would be useful for this. Use a field guide to help you categorize the different insects and other invertebrates into different groups, such as spiders, craneflies, springtails, ants, beetles, moths and butterflies.

## Take it further

* The sundews are my favourite because even though they are small they add a beautiful splash of deep scarlet to any bog. I also love the name as it describes the fact that even in the noon-day sun the leaves still seem to hold the sparkle of early morning dew. It isn't actually dew but a sticky digestive juice. When an insect gets stuck in it, the tentacle-like hairs move towards the prey and slowly digest it. When they straighten up, all that is left of the hapless insect is a dry husk.

* The bright green, fleshy leaves of butterwort remind me of little green starfish, and even though at certain seasons they are topped off by a small but beautiful pink flower, do not be fooled – this is a plant with a dark side. It too has sticky hairs, which ensnare victims and then the whole leaf rolls up around the prey to form a simple stomach. It secretes digestive juice that dissolves and removes all useful compounds from the insect's body.

# Read a reed bed

**A reed bed is probably one of the worst places to see wildlife.** This is ironic really, because reed beds are home to some rather splendid and specialized wildlife! It's just that actually setting your eyes on them is made very difficult by the reeds themselves. But wherever you see the yellow-brown vertically growing stuff, it's always worth a quick look as there are a few things to listen and look out for, especially in the spring and summer.

**Normally spotting things is a little easier than this.** But in reed beds all it takes is a gentle breeze to set the whole environment wafting and waving all over the place. This combined with the dense growth of reeds, which act as a screen, make it almost impossible to simply spot things. But use your ears as well as your eyes and, with a little patience, things can be very different.

**All it takes is for one breath of wind to set the reed bed quivering.**

## Nick's trick

* If you need visual confirmation of what you think you have heard, well, that takes a bit of luck or a length of time. Concentrate on seeing movement, even if it is just a fleeting glimpse of a small brown bird dashing up a dyke. It can give you just enough information to pin a name to the bird.

* Look out, too, for repeated behaviour. Often when a bird is tending a nest it will fly backwards and forwards using the same perches. Get a fix on one of these and you will be in a better position to make the most of a brief glimpse, rather than trying to see it among the reeds.

**Most reed-bed birds give away their presence with sounds**, especially in the breeding season. The birds have just as much difficulty seeing each other in the dense vegetation, so they have to be loud and distinctive to locate each other! Keep your ears open and you could very easily be listening in to the calls of reed, sedge and Cetti's warblers and if you get really lucky, you may hear the 'pinging' of bearded tits or the booming of a bittern. For actual specifics on how to recognize these calls there are many sources of information including brilliant bird call CDs.

**A bittern stretches its long neck high above the reeds.**

# Living sponges

**Boggy places are obviously wet and moist** and many of the plants and creatures that live in them do so because at some time in their lives they need to be damp. One plant more than any other not only creates a habitat for itself but in doing so also becomes the basis for the rest of bog life and this is bog (or sphagnum) moss.

**Bog moss may sound like the definition of dull.** But you'd be wrong. If it wasn't for this plant, we probably wouldn't have upland peat bogs or great rivers that run all year long out of the hills. Peat is the product of slowly decomposing sphagnum moss and some of the most perfectly preserved humans (along with their tools and other soft artefacts) have been recovered from such bogs. In any other habitat, they would have decayed totally. Instead, we have now pulled the semi-mummified remains of several humans from peat bogs – one of the oldest was alive over 5,000 years ago.

**Peat is very familiar to gardeners,** although it is now best to find alternatives to it because of the irreversible damage that peat extraction is doing to our bogs. Sphagnum has also been used as a sterile wound dressing, a water-retaining liner for pots and hanging baskets and indirectly – again as peat – it has been used to fuel fires, warm houses and power industry! Not bad for a soggy moss!

**Sphagnum is a sponge and its presence keeps bogs boggy!** There are many different species, but they nearly all form pretty cushions of lushness, from bright vibrant green to surprising reds and oranges. Touch these cushions formed from lots of closely packed rosettes of leaves, and they are nearly always cold and clammy.

For a simple plant, sphagnum has a huge influence, even when it's dead. It really is like a sponge, holding vast quantities of water, creating bogs and eventually making peat.

**1** Push your hand deep into a clump of sphagnum moss and squish your fingers down as deep as you can. You can feel the way the moss keeps everything cool and holds the moisture.

**2** When you are as deep as you can go, grab a few stems and pull them up and out.

**3** Look at the individual strands of moss. Only the top few centimetres are alive; the rest is dark brown and only at the very deepest part has the stem started to decompose and become peat. It keeps in the water and where it is dark and there is no air and the soil is very acid, decomposition happens very slowly. This is how peat bogs are formed – from the bottom up; even on slopes!

**4** Even after the moss is long dead it continues to benefit the living portions of the plant and its surroundings. It holds water within the special water-retaining cells in the leaves and stems. To see just how effective this is, take your handful of moss and squeeze it between your fingers and watch the water pour out.

# Going further

This book was never meant to be anything but the very beginning of a journey – I see it as being the map, the compass and a pointer in the right direction. As you continue to explore various freshwater habitats, you will begin to ask more questions and discover things that this book may not be able to answer. This is why this section exists.

## Good reading

*Britain's Dragonflies* by Dave Smallshire and Andy Swash (WILDGuides). **A novel and unique photoguide to dragonflies using state-of-the-art digital techniques to bring together all the stages of the lifecycle of each species. Handy if you are trying to identify the nymphs as well as the adults.**

*Frogs and Toads* by Trevor Beebee (Whittet Books). **These little books are often overlooked. OK, they do not have big, glossy pictures but the information contained within the pages and the line drawings all helped by the easy-to-digest** language makes these great books to read from cover to cover and become an instant expert on frogs and toads.

*A Guide to Dragonflies of Great Britain* by Dan Powell (Arlequin Press). **Another great book on this charismatic pond predator but this one takes an entirely different approach, using illustrations to show exactly what you need to be looking for to separate some of the more common species from each other.**

*Illustrated Keys* (Field Studies Council, www.field-studies-council.org). **These** easy-to-use illustrated keys are fantastic and lightweight, contain lots of information and are very cheap at just a few pounds each; there is a huge range of subjects covered.

*The First-time Naturalist* by Nick Baker (Collins) **is a good general guide to all natural habitats.**

## Handy organizations

*Froglife:* **A charity that is all about conserving – well – frogs! Great website that answers all those FAQs about our cold-blooded friends – www.froglife.org.**

*Ponds Trust:* **A charity that is all about ponds and their conservation value. Worth a look if you are serious about yours – www.pondstrust.co.uk.**

*Royal Society for the Protection of Birds (RSPB):* **They really are the big** ones; not only an organization that gives the birds a lot but also the members. Numbers speak for themselves as the RSPB has over a million members. Great magazines too – for adults, kids and teenagers. They produce many handy leaflets with information pertaining specifically to the garden too – www.rspb.org.uk or telephone 01767 680551.

*The Wildlife Trusts:* **They are a countrywide organization and** there will be a regional group near you organizing lots of 'wildlifing' activities for all ages. They produce regular magazines for both grown-ups and younger members and they have a junior wing called Wildlife Watch. This is an organization I would love to have joined when I was a kid but didn't know about, so that's why I'm telling you now – www.wildlifetrusts.org or telephone 0870 0367711.

# Handy stuff – equipment supplies and other contacts

*Alana Ecology:* Everything a naturalist would ever need can be found within the pages of this catalogue. This really is a one-stop shop; if only I could stop shopping there I would be a richer man – www.alanaecoloogy.com or telephone 01588 630173.

*Interplay UK Ltd:* Makers and suppliers of fine educational science-based toys, the most reliable stockist of tadpole shrimps (triops) and the necessary means to culture them – www.interplay.co.uk or telephone 01628 488944.

*Marris House Nets:* Netting, net and net handles! If it goes in a net, they have the net it goes in. No website, but you can telephone 01202 515238.

*Watkins and Doncaster:* These guys have been peddling natural-history collecting and sampling gear for years, I bought my first butterfly net and mammal trap from them when I was a nipper. What they do not know about 'gear' isn't worth knowing – www.watdon.com or telephone 01580 753133.

# Index

# Author's acknowledgements

> Big thanks to the energetic and hard-working team at Harper Collins who put this book together. Especially the tireless Helen Brocklehurst – how she holds everything together when it comes to building books, I don't know. But thankfully she does and she's good at it. And the same for Emma Callery, who as editor for this book has endured the frustrating half-finished manuscripts, bad grammar and spelling and, of course, the continual frustration of not being able to get hold of me on the phone! Thanks for not shouting at me and getting cross! Nikki English, the photographer, who has the patience of a saint and found the energy to continue wrangling animals and children both at the same time AND managing to take great photographs; surely the definition of multi-tasking!

> Edward Jackson and everyone at the Field Studies Council at Flatford; Lizzie Bishop; the RSPB at Aylesbeare; Fingringhoe Wick Nature Reserve; and the fabulous models Aaron, Caitlin, Eddie, George, Hamish, Martha, Megan, Oliver and Sophie.